Mini

File-Folder Centers in Color

SCHOLASTIC

Reading & Writing

12 Irresistible and Easy-to-Make Centers That Help Children Practice
and Strengthen Important Reading and Writing Skills

by Betty Jo Evers

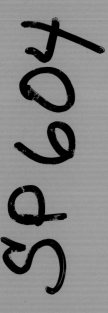

New York • Toronto • London • Auckland • Sydney
Mexico City • New Delhi • Hong Kong • Buenos Aires

Teaching Resources

This book is dedicated to my husband, David (educator and secondary school administrator),
who has provided consistent support and encouragement throughout my teaching career.
Without his guidance, my life as a teacher, presenter, and writer would not have been possible.

Edited by Immacula A. Rhodes
Cover design by Jason Robinson
Interior design by Solas
Cover and interior illustrations by Teresa Anderko, Maxie Chambliss, and Rusty Fletcher

ISBN-13: 978-0-545-17692-7
ISBN-10: 0-545-17692-1

Copyright © 2010 by Betty Jo Evers
Illustrations © 2010 by Scholastic Inc.
Published by Scholastic Inc. All rights reserved. Printed in China.

2 3 4 5 6 7 8 9 10   16 15 14 13 12 11

Contents

Mini File–Folder Centers

About This Book

As teachers, we realize that children learn at different times and in different ways. The desire to help every child succeed leads us to research, learn, and gather information to make teaching as effective as possible. We are constantly in search of ideas and materials that capture children's interest and motivate them to engage in independent reading and writing activities. *Mini File-Folder Centers in Color: Reading & Writing, Grades K–1* was created for just this purpose.

In the 3rd edition of *Best Practice: Today's Standards for Teaching and Learning in America's Schools* by Steven Zemelman, Harvey Daniels, and Arthur Hyde, (Heinemann, 2005), the authors remind us that, "A room with centers offers kids variety in the day, a chance to engage content actively, natural occasions for quiet talk, opportunities for spontaneous collaboration, and the responsibility for making choices." The classroom-tested learning centers in this book give children a fun, engaging way to practice and build skills that help them meet the language arts standards, including the Big Five—phonemic awareness, phonics, vocabulary, comprehension, and fluency—the essential components in the Reading First Program guidelines identified in the *No Child Left Behind Act*. (See "What the Research Says" and "Meeting the Language Arts Standards," page 8, for more.) In addition, the unique mini file-folder format appeals to kids of all learning styles, while the self-checking activities encourage independence and lend support to children who need extra help in reading and writing.

The mini centers are a snap to set up and store: Just cut out the templates, glue them inside file folders that have been cut in half and folded into quarters, and you've got twelve instant centers! The activities are designed to reinforce children's reading and writing skills and include topics such as matching letters, letter-sound relationships, vowels, segmentation, word families, sight words, and more. And they make a great classroom management tool—whether used as anchor activities or sponge activities (exercises that support learning by giving children opportunities to practice, reinforce, or extend skills they already know)—the centers are perfect for individual or partner work, as well as for small-group instruction.

What's Inside

Everything you need for the mini file-folder centers is included in this resource.

Each center activity includes the following:

* an introductory page for the teacher that shows how the center is assembled

* a list of materials needed to prepare and use the activity

* step-by-step assembly directions

* extension activities, including writing activities that continue reinforcing children's skills and interest

* a label with the title of each center for the file-folder tab

* a pocket to attach to the front of the file folder for storing the activity cards

* colorful templates to glue to the inside of the folder

* directions that explain to children how to use the center

* activity cards

* an answer key

Making the Mini File-Folder Centers

Follow these easy directions to prepare the mini file folders and assemble the centers.

How to Prepare the Mini File Folders

1. Cut each extended-tab file folder in half horizontally.

2. Open the folders. Then fold the left side of each mini file folder toward the center fold. Fold it to the right two more times. When finished, you'll have a foldout mini file folder that's divided into four sections by the folds.

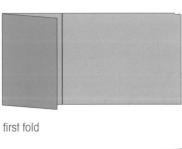

first fold

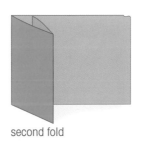

second fold

third fold

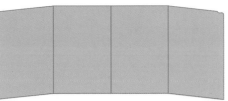

Materials
* 6 extended-tab file folders (in a variety of colors, if available)
* scissors
* glue stick or rubber cement
* craft knife

How to Assemble the Mini File-Folder Centers

1. Glue the center label onto the file-folder tab.

2. With the tab of the folded folder at the right, glue (or tape) the pocket to the front. Glue only along the top, bottom, and left edges of the pocket, leaving the right edge open to serve as the pocket opening.

3. Glue the answer key to the back of the file folder.

4. Open the folder and glue the three templates and directions to the inside sections. (Glue the directions to the far-right section.)

5. Laminate the assembled folder and activity cards for durability. After laminating, use a craft knife to carefully slit open the pocket.

Assembly Tips

* Before cutting the activity cards apart, make additional color or black-and-white copies to have on hand in case pieces are lost.

* To help children keep the activity cards in place when using a center, you might affix self-adhesive Velcro® dots to the inside of the folder and on the back of each card.

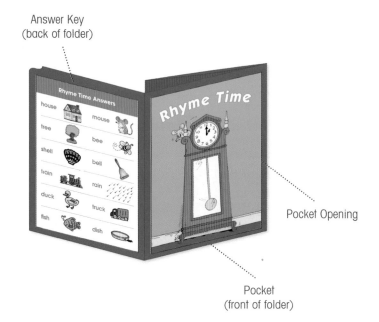

Answer Key
(back of folder)

Pocket Opening

Pocket
(front of folder)

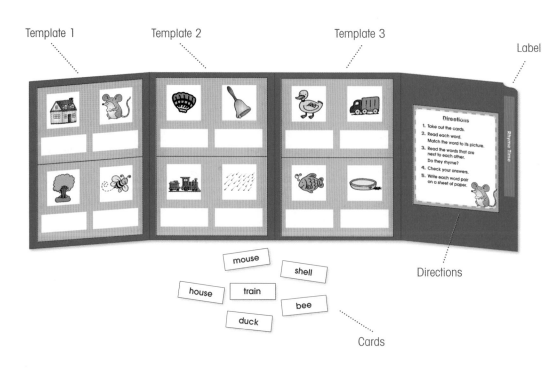

Template 1

Template 2

Template 3

Label

Directions

Cards

Using the Mini File-Folder Centers

❋ Before introducing the centers to children, conduct mini-lessons to review the reading concepts used in each center.

❋ Model for children how to use each center.

❋ Store the mini file-folder activities in a learning center and encourage children to use them for independent learning activities before or after school, during center or free-choice time, when they have finished other tasks, or while you work with other individuals or small groups.

❋ Keep a supply of pencils, markers, and paper available with the centers. Have children complete a writing component for each activity. Some center directions specifically include a step that involves writing, and you'll find additional writing activities in the Extending the Activities section for each center.

❋ When children complete a center, invite them to share their work, including the writing component, with others. Afterward, you might have them place their writing sample in a specified location. You can use their work to track progress and assess skills.

❋ Keep the centers handy for use as quick assessments or for volunteer tutors to use as instructional tools.

❋ Send the mini file-folder centers home with children to give them extra practice and to encourage family involvement in their learning.

One Step Further

Sharing learning is a key component in using the mini file-folder centers. After children complete an activity, provide the time and opportunity for them to share their responses with a friend, partner, small group, or the entire class. When children share what they learn with others, they get further practice in applying their reading and writing skills as they also build vocabulary, communication, and social skills.

Storage Tip

A small shoebox makes an ideal storage container for your mini file-folder centers. You might reinforce the corners of the box and lid with strapping tape for durability, then cover both with decorative paper or vinyl. To prepare for use, set the box inside the lid. Then stand the folders tab end up in the box so children can easily see the labels to find the center they'll work with. For storage after the school year, lay the centers flat in the box and place the lid on top.

What the Research Says

In his book *The Science of Spelling: The Explicit Specifics That Make Great Readers and Writers* (Heinemann, 2004), Richard Gentry states that "When we teach the knowledge needed for spelling to the beginning reader—knowledge about sounds, letter knowledge, concept of what a word is, phonemic awareness, knowledge of the alphabetic principle for mapping spoken language to its printed form, knowledge of spelling patterns (i.e., phonics), and how phonics brings some pattern and consistency to a very complex system for mapping printed language to spoken language—we are teaching the underlying knowledge needed for reading, and for writing."

Meeting the Language Arts Standards

Connections to the McREL Language Arts Standards

Mid-continent Research for Education and Learning (McREL), a nationally recognized nonprofit organization, has compiled and evaluated national and state standards—and proposed what teachers should provide for their K–1 students to grow proficient in reading. The activities in this book support the following standards:

Reading
Uses the general skills and strategies of the reading process including:

- Uses mental images based on pictures and print to aid in comprehension of text
- Uses basic elements of phonetic analysis (common letter-sound relationships, beginning and ending consonants, vowel sounds, word patterns) to decode unknown words
- Uses basic elements of structural analysis (syllables, spelling patterns) to decode unknown words
- Understands level-appropriate sight words and vocabulary

Writing
Uses grammatical and mechanical conventions in written compositions including:

- Uses conventions of print in writing
- Uses complete sentences in written compositions
- Uses conventions of spelling in written compositions
- Uses conventions of capitalization and punctuation in writing

Source: Kendall, J. S., & Marzano, R. J. (2004). *Content knowledge: A compendium of standards and benchmarks for K-12 education.* Aurora, CO: Mid-continent Research for Education and Learning. Online database: http://www.mcrel.org/standards-benchmarks/

Connections to the Reading First Program

The activities in this book are also designed to support you in implementing the Reading First Program, authorized by the U.S. Department of Education's *No Child Left Behind Act.* The National Reading Panel has identified the five key areas of reading instruction as follows:

Phonemic Awareness
The ability to hear, identify, and manipulate phonemes—the sounds of spoken language

Phonics Development
The ability to understand the predictable relationship between phonemes and graphemes—the letters and spellings that represent those sounds in written language—that helps readers recognize familiar words accurately and automatically and to decode unfamiliar words

Vocabulary Development
The ability to store information about the meanings and pronunciation of words necessary for communicating, including vocabulary for listening, speaking, reading, and writing

Fluency
The ability to read text accurately and quickly that allows readers to recognize words and comprehend at the same time

Comprehension
The ability to understand and gain meaning from material read

Source: *Guidance for the Reading First Program.* (U.S. Department of Education Office of Elementary and Secondary Education, 2002).

Letter Match

How to Assemble

1. Cut out the mini file-folder label, pocket, and answer key on page 11. Glue the label onto the file-folder tab. Then glue the top, bottom, and left edges of the pocket to the front of the folder. Glue the answer key to the back of the folder.

2. Cut out the three templates, directions, and letter cards on pages 13 and 15. Open the file folder and glue each template and the directions to the inside sections, as shown. When the center is not in use, store the cards in the pocket on the front of the folder.

Materials

* pages 11–15

* foldout mini file folder

* scissors

* glue

Extending the Activity

To extend learning, instruct children to do the following:

* Match uppercase and lowercase magnetic letters on a magnet board.

* Write each letter and use it in a drawing of something that begins with that letter.

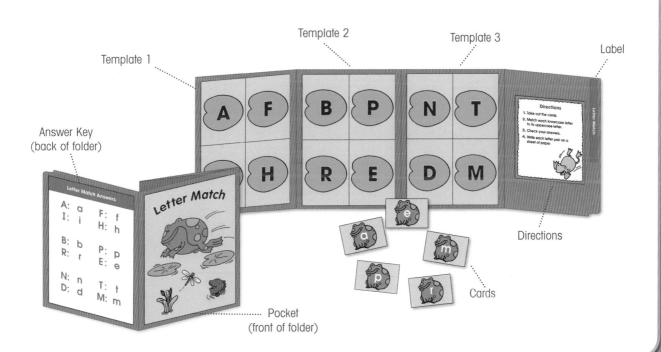

Letter Match

Label

Letter Match

Letter Match Answers

A: a   F: f

I: i   H: h

B: b   P: p

R: r   E: e

N: n   T: t

D: d   M: m

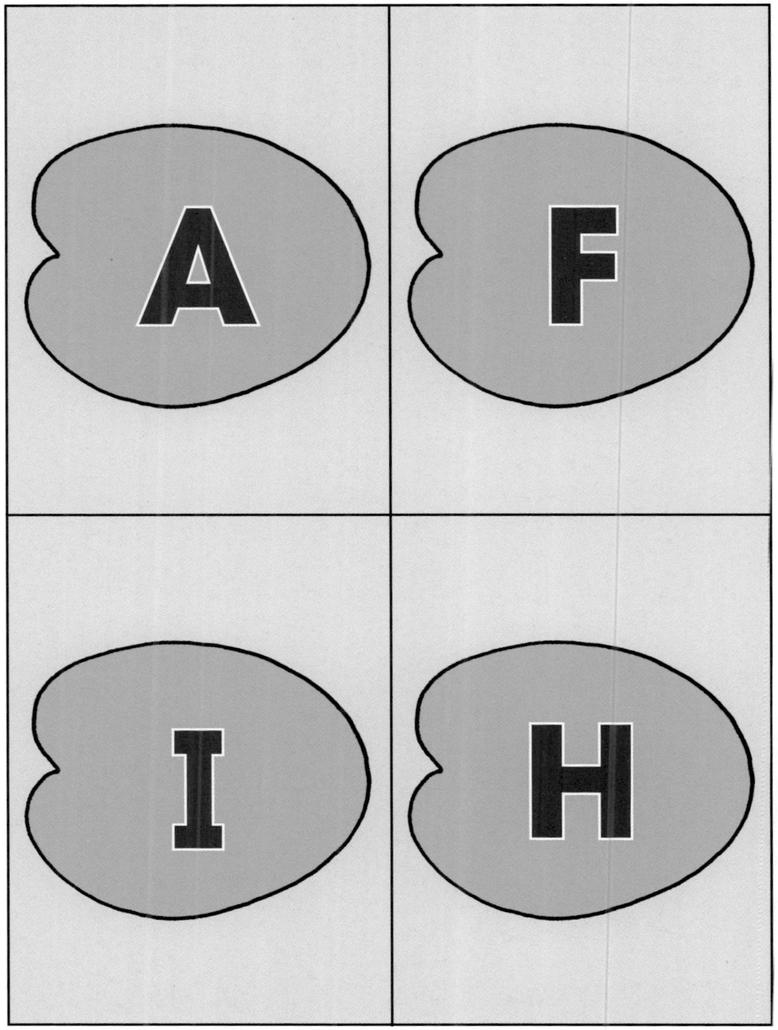

Template 2

P

E

B

R

Template 1

F

H

A

I

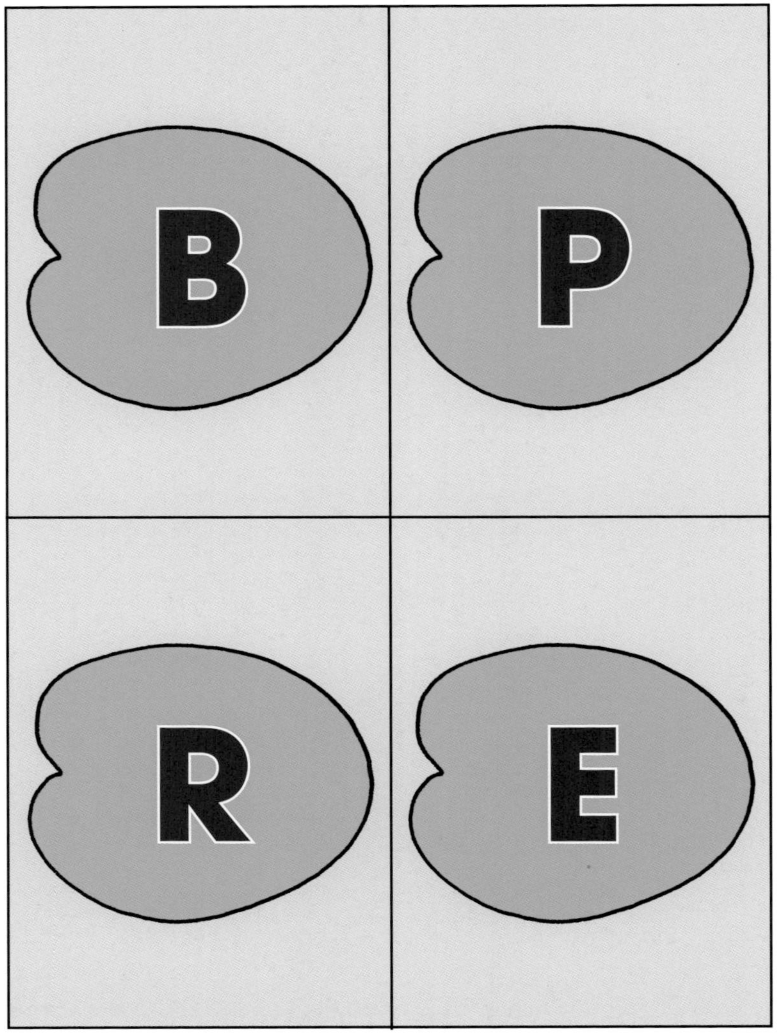

Template 3

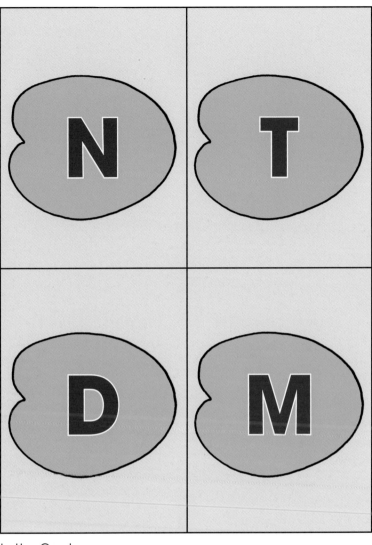

Directions

Directions

1. Take out the cards.

2. Match each lowercase letter to its uppercase letter.

3. Check your answers.

4. Write each letter pair on a sheet of paper.

Letter Cards

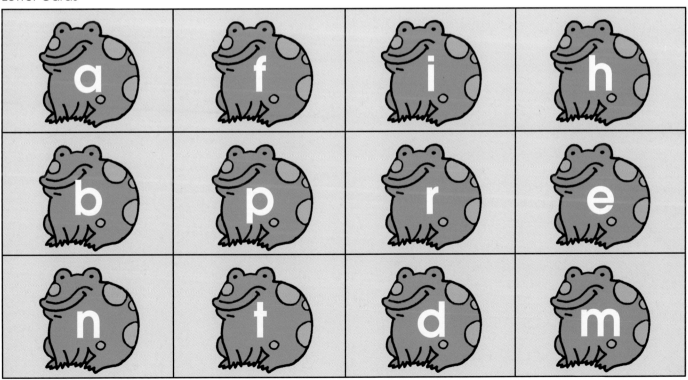

15

Great Beginnings With Bb and Dd

How to Assemble

1. Cut out the mini file-folder label, pocket, and answer key on page 19. Glue the label onto the file-folder tab. Then glue the top, bottom, and left edges of the pocket to the front of the folder. Glue the answer key to the back of the folder.

2. Cut out the three templates, directions, and picture cards on pages 21 and 23. Open the file folder and glue each template and the directions to the inside sections, as shown. When the center is not in use, store the cards in the pocket on the front of the folder.

Materials

✷ pages 19–23

✷ foldout mini file folder

✷ scissors

✷ glue

Extending the Activity

To extend learning, instruct children to do the following:

✷ Draw five things that begin with the sound for each letter: *B* and *D*.

✷ Write the words for the picture cards that begin with *B* on one side of a sheet of paper and those that begin with *D* on the other side.

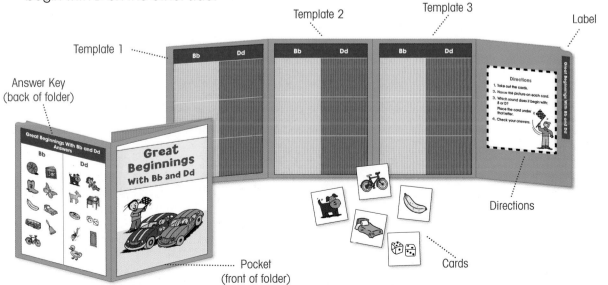

Great Beginnings
With Bb and Dd

Great Beginnings With Bb and Dd

**Great Beginnings With Bb and Dd
Answers**

Dd

Bb

Template 2

	Dd		
Bb			

Template 1

	Dd		
Bb			

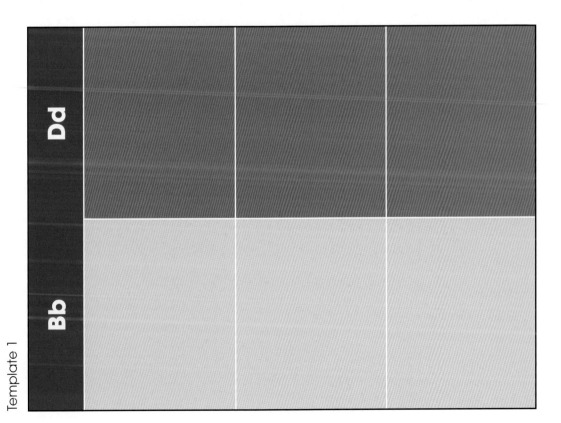

Template 3

Bb	**Dd**

Directions

1. Take out the cards.

2. Name the picture on each card.

3. Which sound does it begin with: B or D?

   Place the card under that letter.

4. Check your answers.

Picture Cards

Sweet Cc Treats

How to Assemble

1. Cut out the mini file-folder label, pocket, and answer key on page 27. Glue the label onto the file-folder tab. Then glue the top, bottom, and left edges of the pocket to the front of the folder. Glue the answer key to the back of the folder.

2. Cut out the three templates, directions, and picture cards on pages 29 and 31. Open the file folder and glue each template and the directions to the inside sections, as shown. When the center is not in use, store the cards in the pocket on the front of the folder.

Materials

* pages 27–31

* foldout mini file folder

* scissors

* glue

Extending the Activity

To extend learning, instruct children to do the following:

* Write the word for each picture card that begins with the hard *C* sound.

* Draw a picture of five other things that begin with the hard *C* sound.

Tip

You might tell children that four picture cards show items that do not begin with the *C* sound.

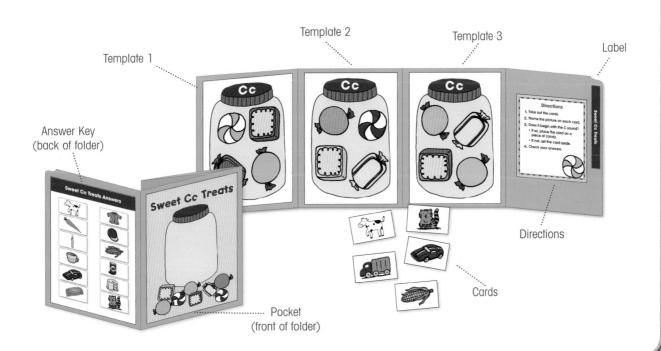

Template 1 — Template 2 — Template 3 — Label

Answer Key (back of folder)

Directions

Cards

Pocket (front of folder)

Sweet Cc Treats

Sweet Cc Treats Answers

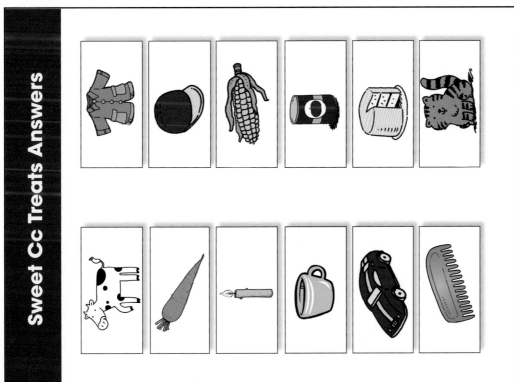

Template 2

Template 1

29

Directions

Directions

1. Take out the cards.

2. Name the picture on each card.

3. Does it begin with the C sound?
   - If so, place the card on a piece of candy.
   - If not, set the card aside.

4. Check your answers.

Picture Cards

Rr and Ww Sound-Sort Webs

How to Assemble

1. Cut out the mini file-folder label, pocket, and answer key on page 35. Glue the label onto the file-folder tab. Then glue the top, bottom, and left edges of the pocket to the front of the folder. Glue the answer key to the back of the folder.

2. Cut out the three templates, directions, and picture cards on pages 37 and 39. Open the file folder and glue each template and the directions to the inside sections, as shown. When the center is not in use, store the cards in the pocket on the front of the folder.

Materials

* pages 35–39
* foldout mini file folder
* scissors
* glue

Extending the Activity

To extend learning, instruct children to do the following:

* Write the words for the picture cards that begin with *R* on one side of a sheet of paper and those that begin with *W* on the other side.

* Group the pictures by whether they are living or nonliving things, then write the words in each group.

Tip

Tell children to stack the cards that they move to the webs.

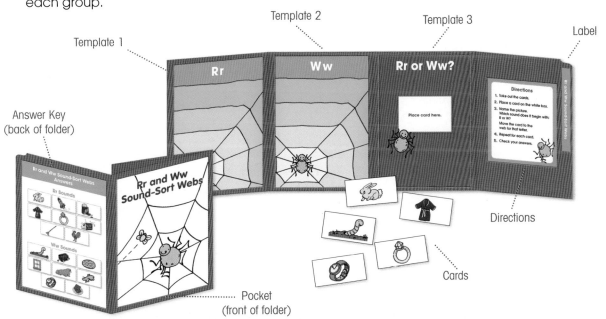

Template 1

Template 2

Template 3

Label

Answer Key
(back of folder)

Directions

Cards

Pocket
(front of folder)

Rr and Ww Sound-Sort Webs

Label

Rr and Ww Sound-Sort Webs

Answers

Rr and Ww Sound-Sort Webs Answers

Rr Sounds

Ww Sounds

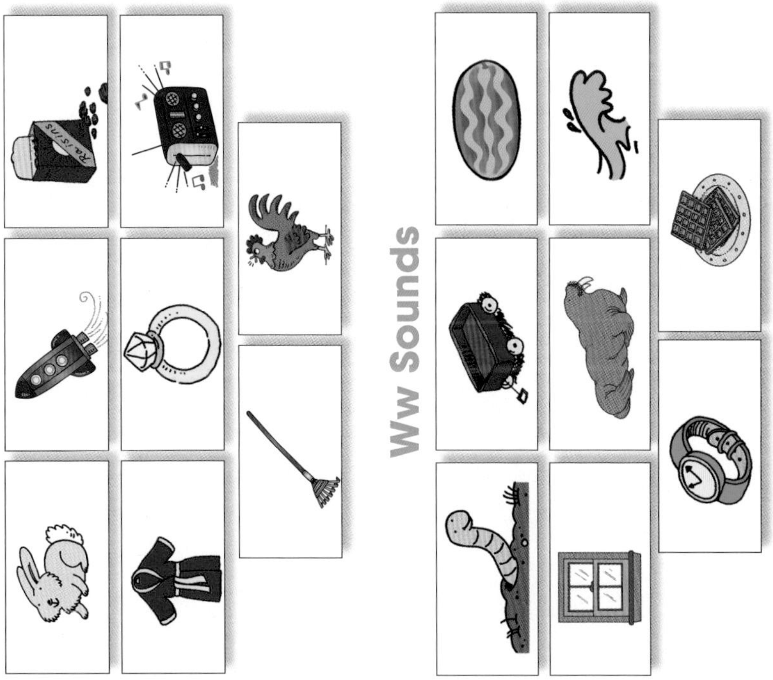

Ww

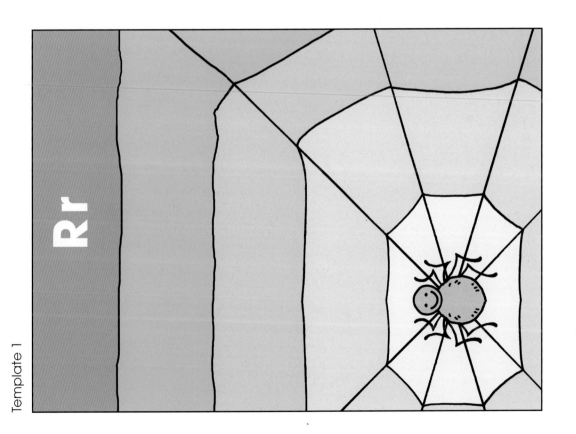

Rr

Rr or Ww?

Place card here.

Directions

1. Take out the cards.

2. Place a card on the white box.

3. Name the picture.
   Which sound does it begin with:
   R or W?
   Move the card to the
   web for that letter.

4. Repeat for each card.

5. Check your answers.

Picture Cards

Short Vowel Sound-Out

How to Assemble

1. Cut out the mini file-folder label, pocket, and answer key on page 43. Glue the label onto the file-folder tab. Then glue the top, bottom, and left edges of the pocket to the front of the folder. Glue the answer key to the back of the folder.

2. Cut out the three templates, directions, and picture cards on pages 45 and 47. Open the file folder and glue each template and the directions to the inside sections, as shown. When the center is not in use, store the cards in the pocket on the front of the folder.

Extending the Activity

To extend learning, instruct children to do the following:

* For each short vowel sound, draw two things (not on the cards) that have that sound in their names.

* Use the spelling frames as models to write other short vowel words, such as *hit*, *hot*, and *hut*.

Materials

* pages 43–47

* foldout mini file folder

* scissors

* glue

* wipe-off pen

* paper towels

Tip

After they complete the center, have children use a paper towel to erase their writing on the file folder.

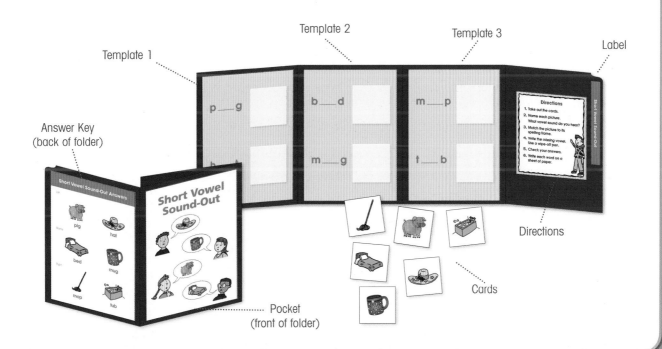

Template 1 · Template 2 · Template 3 · Label · Directions · Cards · Pocket (front of folder) · Answer Key (back of folder)

Short Vowel Sound-Out

Short Vowel Sound-Out

Label

Short Vowel Sound-Out Answers

hat

mug

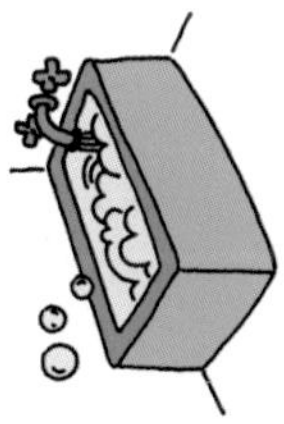

tub

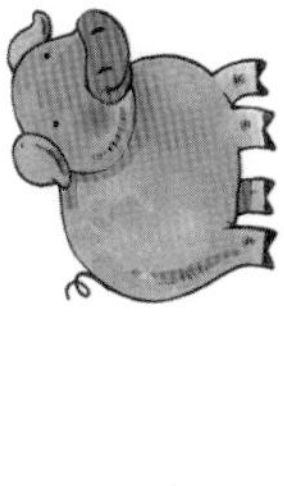

pig

bed

mop

Left:

Middle:

Right:

43

Template 2

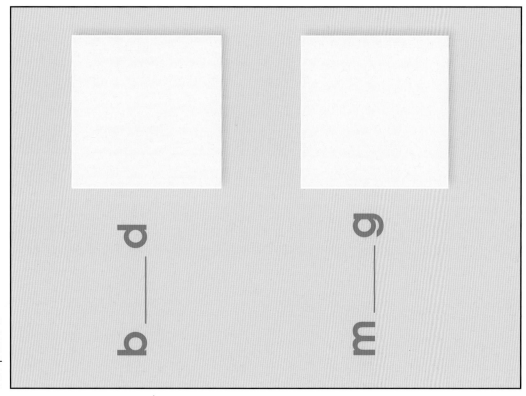

b __ d

m __ g

Template 1

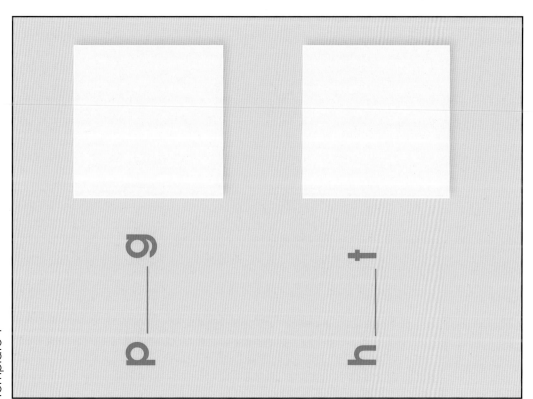

p __ g

h __ t

45

Template 3

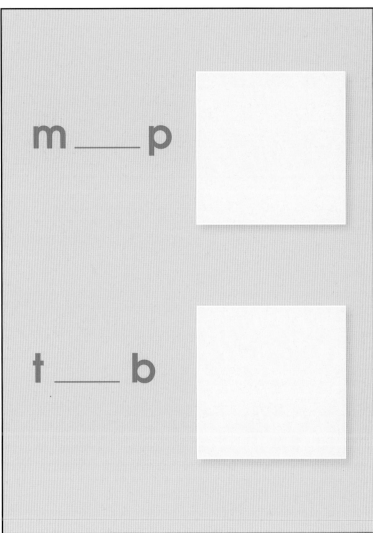

m ___ p

t ___ b

Directions

Directions

1. Take out the cards.

2. Name each picture.
   What vowel sound do you hear?

3. Match the picture to its
   spelling frame.

4. Write the missing vowel.
   Use a wipe-off pen.

5. Check your answers.

6. Write each word on a
   sheet of paper.

Picture Cards

Word-Building With Consonants

How to Assemble

1. Cut out the mini file-folder label, pocket, and answer key on page 51. Glue the label onto the file-folder tab. Then glue the top, bottom, and left edges of the pocket to the front of the folder. Glue the answer key to the back of the folder.

2. Cut out the three templates, directions, and picture cards on pages 53 and 55. Open the file folder and glue each template and the directions to the inside sections, as shown. When the center is not in use, store the cards in the pocket on the front of the folder.

Extending the Activity

To extend learning, instruct children to do the following:

❋ Use the spelling frames as models to write other words that begin and end with consonants, such as *tag*, *leg*, *mix*, *dot*, and *nut*.

❋ Draw pictures to go with as many of their new words as possible.

Materials

✳ pages 51–55

✳ foldout mini file folder

✳ scissors

✳ glue

✳ wipe-off pen

✳ paper towels

Tip

After they complete the center, have children use a paper towel to erase their writing on the file folder.

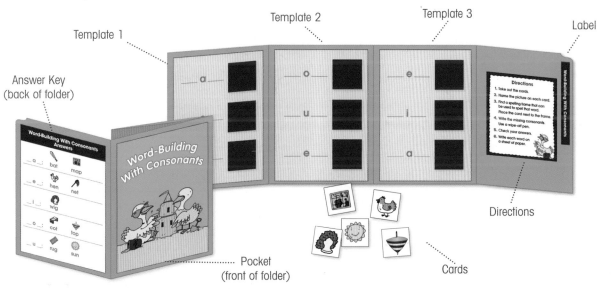

Template 1

Template 2

Template 3

Label

Answer Key
(back of folder)

Directions

Pocket
(front of folder)

Cards

Word-Building With Consonants

Word-Building With Consonants
Answers

__ a __ : map	__ a __ : bat		
__ e __ : net	__ e __ : hen		
__ i __ : wig			
__ o __ : top	__ o __ : cot		
__ u __ : sun	__ u __ : rug		

Template 2

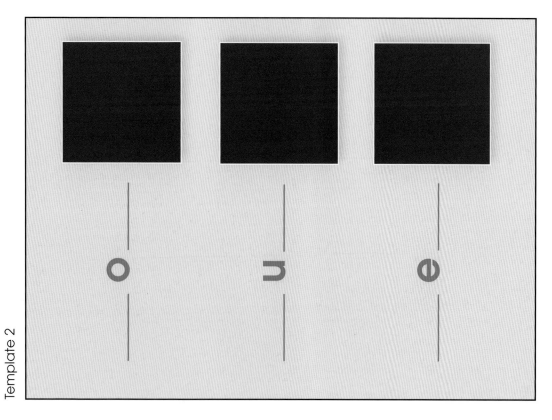

o   u   e

Template 1

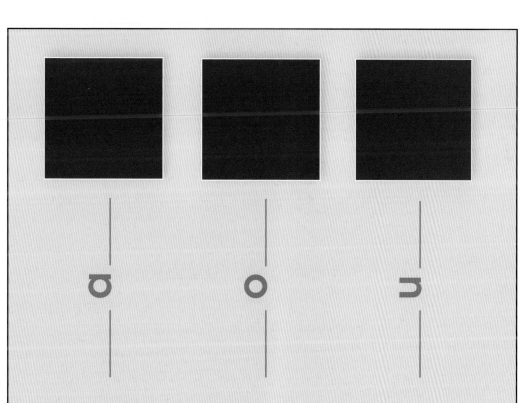

a   o   u

Template 3

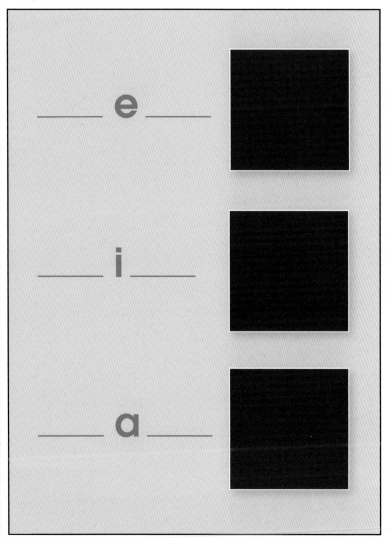

Directions

Directions

1. Take out the cards.

2. Name the picture on each card.

3. Find a spelling frame that can be used to spell that word. Place the card next to the frame.

4. Write the missing consonants. Use a wipe-off pen.

5. Check your answers.

6. Write each word on a sheet of paper.

Picture Cards

Words Sound-by-Sound

How to Assemble

1. Cut out the mini file-folder label, pocket, and answer key on page 59. Glue the label onto the file-folder tab. Then glue the top, bottom, and left edges of the pocket to the front of the folder. Glue the answer key to the back of the folder.

2. Cut out the three templates, directions, and picture cards on pages 61, 63, and 65. Open the file folder and glue each template and the directions to the inside sections, as shown. When the center is not in use, store the cards in the pocket on the front of the folder.

Extending the Activity

To extend learning, instruct children to do the following:

❋ Name each picture and identify the beginning sound of the word.

❋ Draw a picture of ten things. Name each picture and count the sounds in it. Write that number next to the picture.

Materials

✳ pages 59–65

✳ foldout mini file folder

✳ scissors

✳ glue

Tips

• Remind children to say each word sound by sound, counting each sound that they hear. For example, *sun* has three sounds: /s/ /u/ /n/.

• Tell children to stack the cards that they move to the 2-, 3-, and 4-sounds columns.

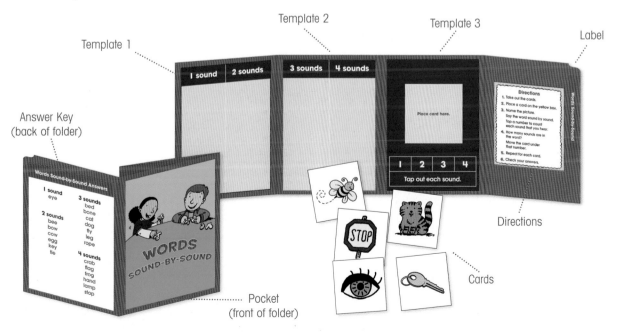

Template 1 · Template 2 · Template 3 · Label

Answer Key (back of folder)

Directions

Cards

Pocket (front of folder)

Pocket

WORDS
SOUND-BY-SOUND

Label

Words Sound-by-Sound

Answers

Words Sound-by-Sound Answers

1 sound
eye

2 sounds
bee
bow
cow
egg
key
tie

3 sounds
bed
bone
cat
dog
fly
leg
rope

4 sounds
crab
flag
frog
hand
lamp
stop

Template 2

4 sounds	3 sounds

Template 1

2 sounds	1 sound

Place card here.

| 1 | 2 | 3 | 4 |

Tap out each sound.

Directions

1. Take out the cards.

2. Place a card on the yellow box.

3. Name the picture.

   Say the word sound by sound.

   Tap a number to count each sound that you hear.

4. How many sounds are in the word?

   Move the card under that number.

5. Repeat for each card.

6. Check your answers.

Picture Cards

Rhyme Time

How to Assemble

1. Cut out the mini file-folder label, pocket, and answer key on page 69. Glue the label onto the file-folder tab. Then glue the top, bottom, and left edges of the pocket to the front of the folder. Glue the answer key to the back of the folder.

2. Cut out the three templates, directions, and word cards on pages 71 and 73. Open the file folder and glue each template and the directions to the inside sections, as shown. When the center is not in use, store the cards in the pocket on the front of the folder.

Materials

❋ pages 69–73

❋ foldout mini file folder

❋ scissors

❋ glue

Extending the Activity

To extend learning, instruct children to do the following:

❋ On their paper, write one more word that rhymes with each pair of words and uses the same spelling pattern.

❋ Use each pair of rhyming words in a sentence.

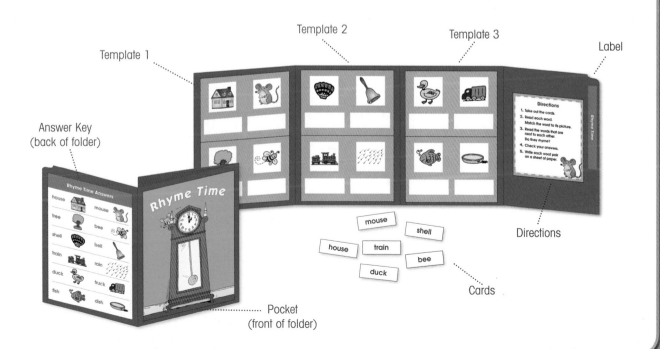

Pocket

Rhyme Time

Rhyme Time

Label

Answers

Rhyme Time Answers

mouse	house		
bee	tree		
bell	shell		
rain	train		
truck	duck		
dish	fish		

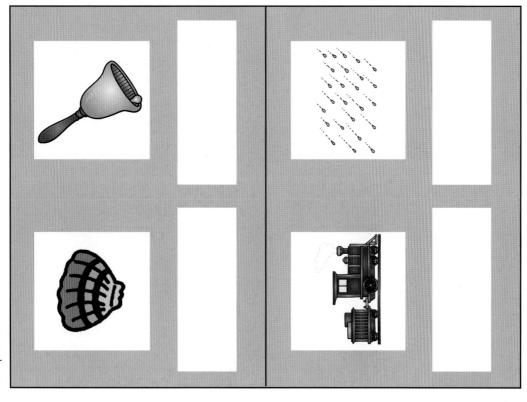

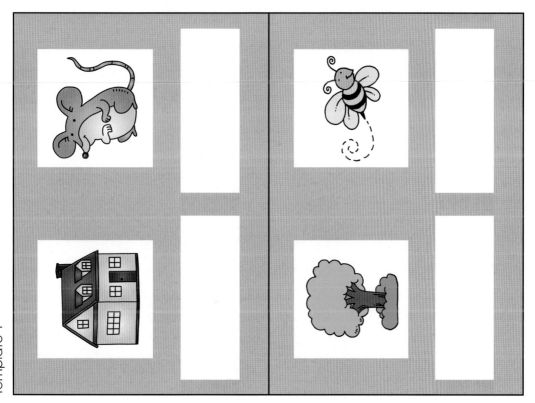

Template 3

Directions

1. Take out the cards.

2. Read each word.
   Match the word to its picture.

3. Read the words that are next to each other.
   Do they rhyme?

4. Check your answers.

5. Write each word pair on a sheet of paper.

Word Cards

house	mouse	tree	bee
shell	bell	train	rain
duck	truck	fish	dish

Wonderful Color Words

How to Assemble

1. Cut out the mini file-folder label, pocket, and answer key on page 77. Glue the label onto the file-folder tab. Then glue the top, bottom, and left edges of the pocket to the front of the folder. Glue the answer key to the back of the folder.

2. Cut out the three templates, directions, and word cards on pages 79, 81, and 83. Open the file folder and glue each template and the directions to the inside sections, as shown. When the center is not in use, store the cards in the pocket on the front of the folder.

Extending the Activity

To extend learning, instruct children to do the following:

✳ Use magnetic letters to spell out the color words on a magnet board.

✳ Write each color word on a sheet of paper using a matching colored marker.

Materials

✳ pages 77–83

✳ foldout mini file folder

✳ scissors

✳ glue

Tip

Use only one set of word cards in the center, starting with the cards printed in color. When children become familiar with the words and their shapes and meanings, replace the colored words with those printed in black.

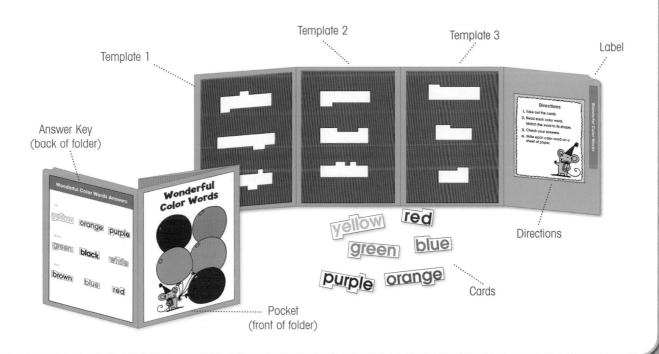

Template 1
Template 2
Template 3
Label

Answer Key
(back of folder)

Directions

Cards

Pocket
(front of folder)

Wonderful Color Words

Label

Wonderful Color Words

Wonderful Color Words Answers

Left: **yellow** **orange** **purple**

Middle: **green** **black** **white**

Right: **brown** **blue** **red**

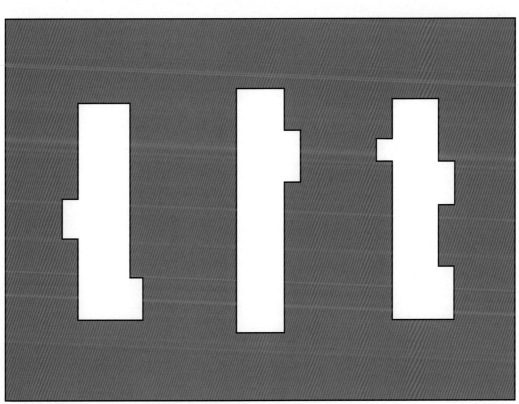

Template 3

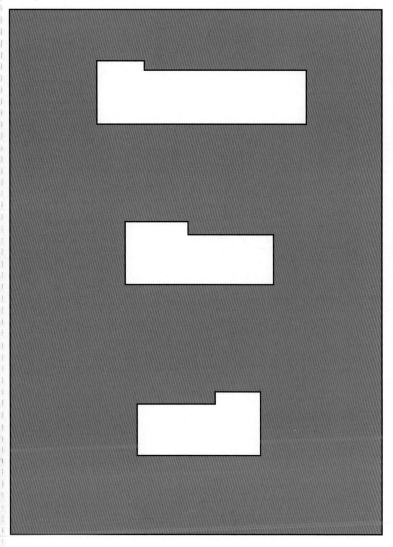

Directions

Directions

1. Take out the cards.

2. Read each color word. Match the word to its shape.

3. Check your answers.

4. Write each color word on a sheet of paper.

Word Cards

red

blue

black

brown

green

white

orange

purple

yellow

Extra Cards

red

blue

black

brown

green

white

orange

purple

yellow

Out-of-This-World Number Words

How to Assemble

1. Cut out the mini file-folder label, pocket, and answer key on page 87. Glue the label onto the file-folder tab. Then glue the top, bottom, and left edges of the pocket to the front of the folder. Glue the answer key to the back of the folder.

2. Cut out the three templates, directions, and word cards on pages 89 and 91. Open the file folder and glue each template and the directions to the inside sections, as shown. When the center is not in use, store the cards in the pocket on the front of the folder.

Materials

* pages 87–91

* foldout mini file folder

* scissors

* glue

Extending the Activity

To extend learning, instruct children to do the following:

* Use magnetic letters on a magnet board (or letter tiles on a tabletop) to spell out each number word.

* Have a partner use the word cards to check their spelling as they spell out each number word.

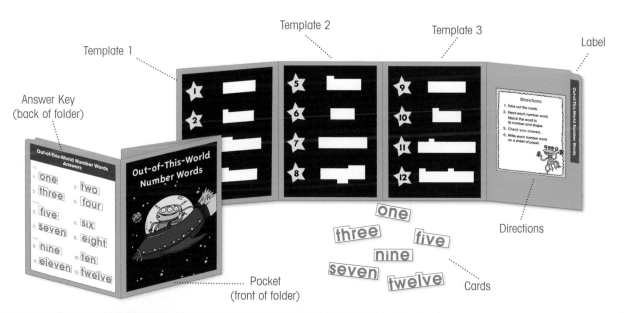

Template 1 Template 2 Template 3 Label

Answer Key (back of folder)

Pocket (front of folder)

Directions

Cards

Pocket

Label

Out-of-This-World Number Words

Answers

Out-of-This-World Number Words
Answers

Left:		Middle:		Right:	
1: **one**	2: **two**	5: **five**	6: **six**	9: **nine**	10: **ten**
3: **three**	4: **four**	7: **seven**	8: **eight**	11: **eleven**	12: **twelve**

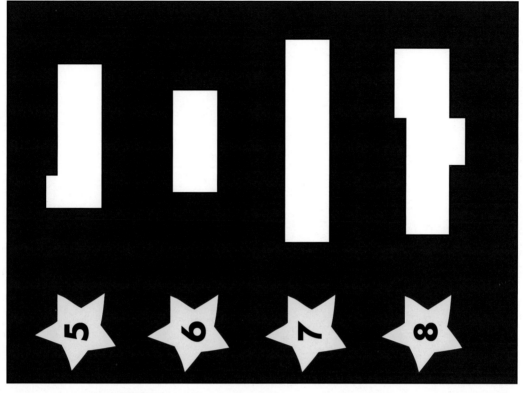

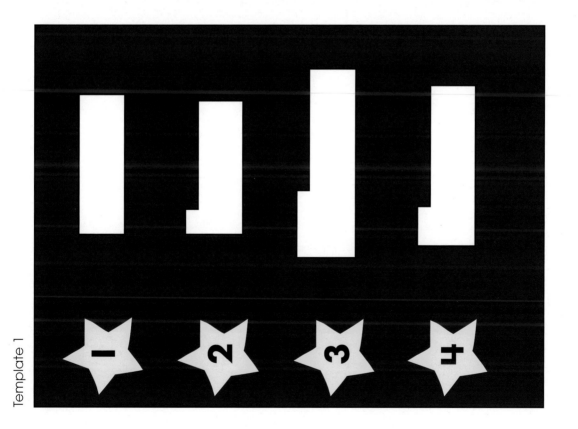

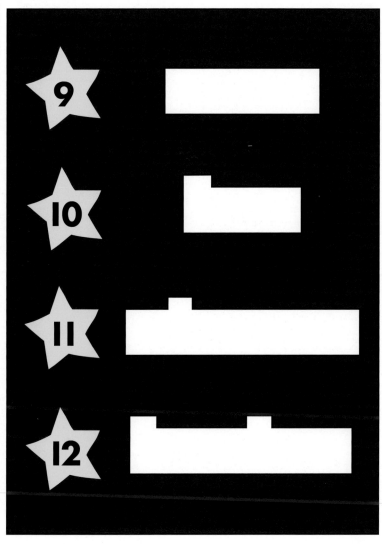

Directions

1. Take out the cards.

2. Read each number word. Match the word to its number and shape.

3. Check your answers.

4. Write each number word on a sheet of paper.

Word Cards

one two three

four five six

seven eight nine

ten eleven twelve

Sight-Word Speed Read

How to Assemble

1. Cut out the mini file-folder label, pocket, and answer key on page 95. Glue the label onto the file-folder tab. Then glue the top, bottom, and left edges of the pocket to the front of the folder. Glue the answer key to the back of the folder.

2. Cut out the three templates, directions, and word cards on pages 97, 99, and 101. Open the file folder and glue each template and the directions to the inside sections, as shown. When the center is not in use, store the cards in the pocket on the front of the folder.

Extending the Activity

To extend learning, instruct children to do the following:

❋ Write the sight words from the center on index cards. Take the cards home to practice reading the words.

❋ Have a partner use the word cards to check their spelling as they spell out each word.

Materials

❋ pages 95–101

❋ foldout mini file folder

❋ scissors

❋ glue

❋ kitchen timer

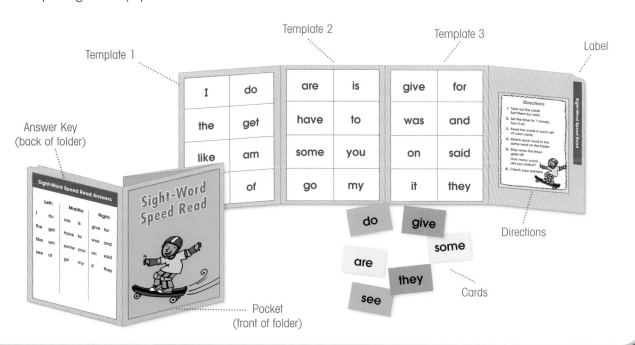

Template 1 · Template 2 · Template 3 · Label

I	do
the	get
like	am
	of

are	is
have	to
some	you
go	my

give	for
was	and
on	said
it	they

Directions

Answer Key (back of folder)

Sight-Word Speed Read Answers

Left:		Middle:		Right:	
I	do	are	is	give	for
the	get	have	to	was	and
like	am	some	you	on	said
see	of	go	my	it	they

Sight-Word Speed Read

do · give · some · are · they · see · Cards

Pocket (front of folder)

Sight-Word Speed Read

Sight-Word Speed Read

Sight-Word Speed Read Answers

Left:		Middle:		Right:	
I	do	are	is	give	for
the	get	have	to	was	and
like	am	some	you	on	said
see	of	go	my	it	they

is	are
to	have
you	some
my	go

do	I
get	the
am	like
of	see

give	for
was	and
on	said
it	they

Directions

1. Take out the cards.
   Sort them by color.

2. Set the timer to 1 minute.
   Turn it on.

3. Read the words in each set
   of color cards.

4. Match each word to the
   same word on the folder.

5. Stop when the timer
   goes off.

   How many words
   did you match?

6. Check your answers.

Word Cards

I	do	the	get
like	am	see	of
are	is	have	some
to	you	go	my
give	for	was	and
they	said	it	on

Looking Out for One or More

How to Assemble

1. Cut out the mini file-folder label, pocket, and answer key on page 105. Glue the label onto the file-folder tab. Then glue the top, bottom, and left edges of the pocket to the front of the folder. Glue the answer key to the back of the folder.

2. Cut out the three templates, directions, and picture cards on pages 107, 109, and 111. Open the file folder and glue each template and the directions to the inside sections, as shown. When the center is not in use, store the cards in the pocket on the front of the folder.

Materials

* pages 105–111

* foldout mini file folder

* scissors

* glue

Extending the Activity

To extend learning, instruct children to do the following:

* Use magnetic letters on a magnet board to spell each singular word. Add *s* to make it plural.

* Write a sentence with each singular word. Then rewrite the sentence with its plural form.

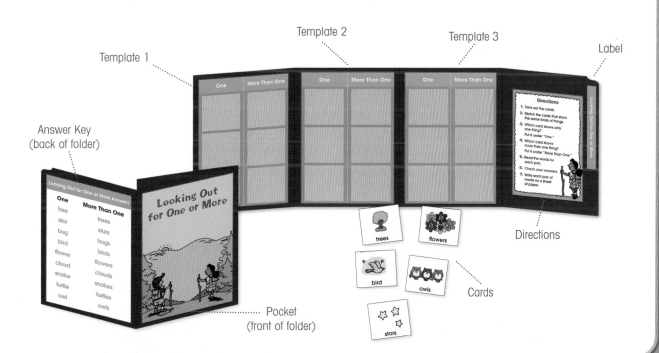

Template 1

Template 2

Template 3

Label

Answer Key
(back of folder)

Directions

Cards

Pocket
(front of folder)

Looking Out for One or More

Label

Looking Out for One or More

Answers

Looking Out for One or More Answers

One	More Than One
tree	trees
star	stars
bug	bugs
bird	birds
flower	flowers
cloud	clouds
snake	snakes
turtle	turtles
owl	owls

Template 2

One	More Than One

Template 1

One	More Than One

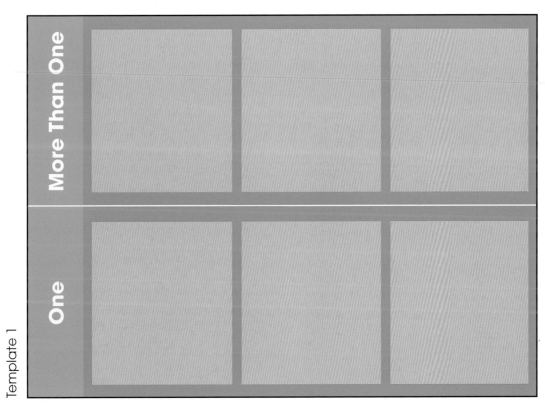

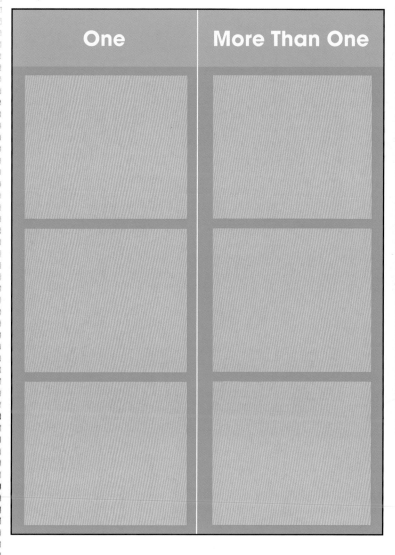

One	More Than One

Directions

1. Take out the cards.

2. Match the cards that show the same kinds of things.

3. Which card shows only one thing?
   Put it under "One."

4. Which card shows more than one thing?
   Put it under "More Than One."

5. Read the words for each pair.

6. Check your answers.

7. Write each pair of words on a sheet of paper.

Picture Cards

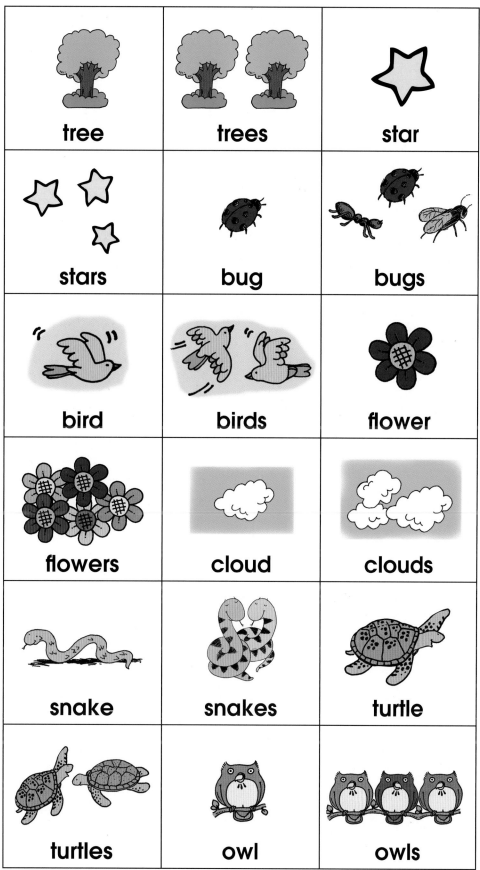

tree	trees	star
stars	bug	bugs
bird	birds	flower
flowers	cloud	clouds
snake	snakes	turtle
turtles	owl	owls